AMANPREET KAUR

How to Start a Small Business from Home

Mastering the Art of Home-Based Entrepreneurship

Rana Books

Contents

Introduction

Introduction: Starting a small business from home has become an increasingly popular and viable option for entrepreneurs in recent years. Advances in technology, changes in work culture, and the desire for greater flexibility have all contributed to the rise of home-based businesses. This approach offers numerous advantages, such as reduced overhead costs, convenience, and the ability to blend personal and professional life. However, it also presents its own set of challenges that require careful planning and execution.

In this guide, we will explore the fundamental aspects of starting a small business from home. From ideation to implementation, we will cover the key steps and considerations that aspiring entrepreneurs need to keep in mind as they embark on this journey. Whether you're looking to turn a hobby into a source of income or you have a unique business idea, this guide will provide valuable insights to help you succeed.

1. Finding Your Business Idea:
    The first step in starting a home-based business is identifying a viable business idea. This could involve capitalizing on your existing skills, pursuing a passion, or spotting a gap in the

market. Research and brainstorming will help you refine your idea and ensure it has the potential to meet a demand or solve a problem.

2. Market Research:

Once you've settled on a business idea, conduct thorough market research. Understand your target audience, analyze competitors, and assess the demand for your product or service. This information will guide your business strategy and help you tailor your offerings to the needs of your potential customers.

3. Business Planning:

Creating a comprehensive business plan is crucial. Outline your business goals, strategies, financial projections, and marketing plans. A well-thought-out business plan not only serves as a roadmap for your business but is also often required if you seek financing or investors.

4. Legal and Regulatory Considerations:

Running a home-based business involves legal considerations. Register your business, obtain any necessary licenses or permits, and understand zoning regulations that might apply to your area. It's important to differentiate between your personal and business finances for tax purposes.

5. Setting Up Your Home Workspace:

Designate a dedicated space within your home for your business activities. This space should be organized, comfortable, and conducive to productivity. Consider factors like lighting, ergonomics, and the equipment you'll need.

6. Building an Online Presence:

In today's digital age, establishing an online presence is essential. Create a professional website, set up social media profiles, and develop an effective online marketing strategy to reach your target audience.

7. Time Management and Work-Life Balance:

Working from home requires effective time management to avoid burnout and ensure that your personal and professional lives remain balanced. Set clear work hours, establish routines, and create boundaries to maintain your overall well-being.

8. Scaling and Growth:

As your home-based business gains traction, you might consider scaling and expanding. This could involve hiring employees, outsourcing tasks, or even transitioning to a physical location if it aligns with your business goals.

Starting a small business from home can be a rewarding endeavor, but it requires careful planning, dedication, and a willingness to adapt to changing circumstances. This guide will provide you with valuable insights and practical tips to navigate the exciting journey of building and growing your home-based business.

1. Flexibility: One of the biggest advantages of starting a small business from home is the flexibility it offers. You have the freedom to set your own working hours and create a work-life balance that suits your needs. This can be particularly beneficial for those with personal commitments or obligations.

Example: Sarah is a stay-at-home mom who wants to start her own baking business. By running her business from home she can manage her work hours around her children's schedule ensuring she can still be actively involved in their lives while pursuing her entrepreneurial dreams.

2. Reduced Overhead Costs: Operating a business from home eliminates the need for a separate office or retail space thereby significantly reducing overhead costs. You can save money on rent utilities and commuting expenses enabling you to invest more in your business or enjoy higher profit margins.

Example: John is an artist who chooses to sell his artwork online from his home. By avoiding the expenses associated with renting a gallery space he can price his artworks more competitively and attract a larger customer base resulting in higher sales.

3. Increased Work-Life Balance: Starting a small business from home allows you to integrate your personal and professional life more seamlessly. You can save valuable time by eliminating the daily commute and you have the flexibility to handle personal responsibilities while still attending to your business needs.

Example: Maria is a freelance graphic designer who runs her business from home. She can easily take breaks during the day to spend time with her family or pursue personal interests knowing that she has the flexibility to make up for the lost time later.

4. Tax Deductions: Operating a small business from home can offer potential tax deductions. Certain expenses such as a

portion of your mortgage or rent utilities and office supplies may be deductible as business expenses. Consulting with a tax professional can help you maximize these deductions and potentially save money.

Example: David runs his online marketing consultancy from his home office. He can deduct a portion of his monthly rent utilities and even a portion of his internet bill as business expenses effectively reducing his taxable income.

1.2 Factors to Consider Before Starting a Small Business from Home:

1. Legal and Zoning Regulations: Before starting a small business from home it is crucial to research and understand the legal and zoning regulations in your area. Some neighborhoods or municipalities may have restrictions or regulations that prohibit or limit certain types of businesses from operating from residential properties.

Example: Lisa wants to start a daycare center from her home but discovers that her neighborhood's zoning regulations do not permit such businesses. She must either find an alternative location or consider a different business idea.

2. Distractions and Boundaries: Working from home can present unique distractions such as household chores family members or personal commitments. It is important to establish clear boundaries and create a dedicated workspace to minimize distractions and maintain focus on your business.

Example: Michael starts a small e-commerce business from his home but finds it challenging to stay productive due to constant interruptions from his roommates. To overcome this he sets aside specific work hours communicates his boundaries with his roommates and creates a designated workspace where he can focus.

3. Market Accessibility: Depending on the nature of your business operating from home may limit your accessibility to certain markets. If your business relies heavily on foot traffic or requires a physical presence consider whether your home location aligns with your target market or if it would be more beneficial to explore alternative options.

Example: Amanda wants to start a boutique clothing store but lives in a residential area with limited foot traffic. Instead of opening her store from home she decides to rent a storefront in a more commercial area to attract a larger customer base.

4. Professional Image: Depending on your business and industry operating from home may impact the perception of professionalism from potential clients or customers. Consider whether having a dedicated office space outside of your home or utilizing virtual office services would be more suitable for your target market.

Example: James is a financial advisor and decides to start his practice from home. However he quickly realizes that potential clients are more likely to trust established financial firms with a brick-and-mortar presence. He rents a small office space to enhance his professional image and credibility.

Identifying Your Business Idea

One of the most crucial and exciting steps in the entrepreneurial journey is identifying a business idea that holds promise and potential. The process of finding the right business idea involves a combination of creativity, market awareness, problem-solving, and a deep understanding of your own skills and passions. Whether you're looking to start a small venture from home or aiming for a larger-scale enterprise, the foundation of your success lies in selecting the right business concept.

In this guide, we will delve into the art and science of identifying a viable business idea. We'll explore techniques to uncover opportunities, strategies to validate your concepts, and considerations to ensure that your chosen idea aligns with your goals and the market's demands.

1.1 The Benefits of Starting a Small Business from Home

1. Self-Assessment:

The journey begins with introspection. What are your skills, strengths, and areas of expertise? What passions or interests do you have? Combining your abilities with your personal interests can lead to a business idea that not only capitalizes on your strengths but also keeps you motivated and engaged.

2. Identifying Market Gaps:

Entrepreneurial success often comes from identifying problems that need solving. Look for gaps in the market—needs or challenges that are currently underserved or overlooked. This could involve conducting market research to uncover unmet demands or exploring industries where innovation is lacking.

3. Leveraging Trends:

Keeping an eye on current trends and emerging technologies can spark innovative business ideas. Whether it's related to technology, sustainability, health, or lifestyle, adapting to evolving trends can position your business idea at the forefront of a changing landscape.

4. Solving Problems:

Businesses that offer solutions to real problems tend to thrive. Consider the pain points people experience in their daily lives and think about how you can address them with a product or service. Problem-solving business ideas often have built-in demand.

5. Passion Projects:

Sometimes, turning a hobby or a passion into a business can be incredibly rewarding. If you're enthusiastic about something, chances are there are others who share your passion and might be interested in what you offer.

6. Market Research:

Conduct thorough research to validate your business idea.

Study your target audience, understand their preferences, and assess the competition. This step will help you refine your concept and tailor it to the needs of potential customers.

7. Innovation and Uniqueness:

Aim to stand out from the crowd by offering something unique. Whether it's a novel twist on an existing concept or a completely original idea, innovation can capture attention and set your business apart.

8. Feasibility and Resources:

Consider the resources you have available—financial, time, and skills. Your business idea should align with your available resources to ensure a realistic and sustainable venture.

9. Adaptability and Growth Potential:

Evaluate whether your chosen business idea has room for growth and adaptability. A successful idea should have the potential to evolve with changing market dynamics and customer preferences.

Identifying the right business idea is the foundation upon which your entrepreneurial journey is built. By combining your strengths, interests, and market insights, you can uncover an idea that not only resonates with you but also has the potential to meet a genuine need and create value. This guide will walk you through the process of discovering and refining your business idea, setting you on a path toward entrepreneurial success.

2.1 Assessing Your Skills Passion and Expertise:

When it comes to identifying a business idea one of the first steps is to assess your skills passion and expertise. This is important because starting a business requires a certain level of knowledge and expertise in a particular area. Here are some steps to help you assess your skills passion and expertise:

1. Make a list of your skills and strengths: Start by making a list of your skills talents and strengths. These could be anything from marketing and sales skills to technical skills or creative skills. Think about your past experiences education and training to identify the areas where you excel.

For example if you have a background in graphic design and enjoy creating visually appealing content you could consider starting a graphic design studio or freelancing in that field.

2. Identify your passions and interests: Consider what you are passionate about and genuinely interested in. This can be a key driver for your business idea as it will keep you motivated and engaged in your work. It's important to have a genuine interest in the industry or field you choose to pursue.

For instance if you are passionate about fitness and have experience in personal training you may consider opening a fitness studio or becoming a personal trainer.

3. Evaluate your expertise and experience: Assess the expertise and experience you have gained in your career education or personal life. Look for areas where you have significant knowledge and expertise. This can provide you with a competitive advantage in the market.

For example if you have worked in the hospitality industry for several years and have extensive knowledge of hotel operations you could consider starting a consultancy or management company that helps hotel owners improve their businesses.

4. Consider your transferable skills: Think about the skills you have that can be applied across different industries or sectors. These transferable skills can open up a wide range of business ideas for you. Some examples of transferable skills include communication problem-solving leadership and project management.

For instance if you have excellent communication skills and enjoy working with people you could consider starting a coaching or consulting business where you help individuals or organizations improve their communication skills.

Once you have assessed your skills passion and expertise you can move on to the next step in identifying your business idea.

2.2 Researching Market Demand and Competition:

Researching market demand and competition is a crucial step in identifying a viable business idea. It helps you understand the potential demand for your product or service and allows you to assess the level of competition in the market. Here are some steps to help you research market demand and competition:

1. Identify your target market: Start by defining your target market. Who are your potential customers? What are their needs preferences and pain points? Understanding your target market

will help you tailor your business idea to meet their specific needs.

For example if your target market consists of busy professionals who struggle to find healthy meal options you may consider starting a meal delivery service that offers nutritious and convenient meals.

2. Conduct market research: Once you have identified your target market conduct thorough market research to gather valuable insights. This can involve analyzing industry reports conducting surveys or interviews and studying consumer trends.

For instance if you are considering starting an e-commerce business you can research the current e-commerce market identify popular product categories and understand customer preferences.

3. Assess market demand: Use the information gathered from your market research to assess the demand for your product or service. Look for any gaps or unmet needs in the market that your business idea can address.

For example if you find that there is a growing demand for eco-friendly home products you could consider starting an online store specializing in sustainable and eco-friendly home goods.

4. Analyze the competition: Research and analyze your competitors to understand their strengths weaknesses and market positioning. This will help you identify opportunities for differentiation and competitive advantage.

For instance if there are already several coffee shops in your area you could consider opening a specialty coffee shop that focuses on high-quality beans and unique brewing methods to differentiate yourself from the competition.

Researching market demand and competition is an ongoing process. It's important to stay up to date with industry trends consumer preferences and the competitive landscape to ensure the long-term viability of your business idea.

2.3 Brainstorming and Narrowing Down Your Business Idea:

Brainstorming and narrowing down your business idea is the final step in the process of identifying a business idea. This step involves generating a wide range of ideas evaluating their feasibility and selecting the most promising ones. Here are some steps to help you brainstorm and narrow down your business idea:

1. Generate a list of ideas: Start by generating a list of business ideas based on your skills passion expertise and market research. Don't limit yourself at this stage and let your creativity flow. Write down as many ideas as possible regardless of how feasible they may seem.

For example if you have a background in technology and are passionate about sustainability you could consider developing a mobile app that helps individuals track their carbon footprint and make more sustainable lifestyle choices.

2. Evaluate feasibility: Once you have a list of ideas evaluate their

feasibility by considering factors such as startup costs resources required market demand competition and your own capabilities. Eliminate ideas that seem unrealistic or beyond your reach at the current stage.

For instance if you have limited financial resources and find that starting a brick-and-mortar store requires a significant investment you may consider exploring online business models that have lower startup costs.

3. Consider your unique selling proposition: Identify the unique selling proposition (USP) for each of your remaining business ideas. A USP is what sets your business apart from the competition and gives you a competitive advantage. It could be offering a unique product targeting a specific niche providing exceptional customer service or using innovative technology.

For example if you are considering starting a clothing brand your USP could be using sustainable and ethically sourced materials appealing to environmentally conscious consumers.

4. Test and validate your business idea: Before fully committing to a business idea consider testing and validating it. This can involve conducting a small-scale pilot or launching a minimum viable product (MVP) to gather feedback from early adopters. Use this feedback to refine your idea and make any necessary adjustments.

For instance if you are developing a new mobile app you could release a beta version to a select group of users and gather their feedback on usability features and overall satisfaction. This will help you identify areas for improvement before launching the app to a wider audience.

5. Make a final decision: After evaluating your ideas considering their feasibility and validating your top choices make a final decision on the business idea you want to pursue. Consider factors such as your passion the market potential your skills and resources and the long-term sustainability of the idea.

For example if you find that there is a high demand for personal-ized pet accessories you have a passion for pets and you have the necessary skills to design and produce these accessories you may decide to start an online business specializing in custom-made pet products.

In conclusion identifying a business idea involves assessing your skills passion and expertise researching market demand and competition and brainstorming and narrowing down your ideas. It's a multi-step process that requires careful consideration and evaluation. By following these steps you can increase your chances of finding a viable and sustainable business idea that aligns with your interests and goals.

Conducting a Feasibility Study

Assessing Viability and Making Informed Decisions

A feasibility study is a critical process undertaken by businesses, organizations, and individuals to determine the viability and potential success of a proposed project or initiative. It serves as a structured analysis that assesses various aspects, such as technical, financial, operational, legal, and environmental, to provide a comprehensive understanding of whether the project is worth pursuing. Conducting a feasibility study helps stakeholders make informed decisions by identifying potential challenges, risks, and opportunities associated with the project.

Key Components of a Feasibility Study:

1. Market Feasibility: This component evaluates the demand for the product or service the project aims to offer. It involves researching the target market, understanding customer needs, analyzing competition, and identifying potential customer segments. By gauging market interest, the feasibility study determines if there is a viable market for the project.

2. Technical Feasibility: This aspect assesses whether the

proposed project is technically possible given the available resources and technology. It considers factors such as required equipment, infrastructure, technology capabilities, and any potential technical obstacles that may arise during project implementation.

3. Financial Feasibility: The financial component analyzes the economic viability of the project. It involves estimating the initial investment costs, ongoing operational expenses, revenue projections, and potential return on investment (ROI). Financial feasibility helps stakeholders determine if the project is financially sustainable and if the anticipated returns justify the investment.

4. Operational Feasibility: This assessment examines whether the project can be smoothly integrated into the existing operations of the organization. It considers factors such as the availability of skilled personnel, necessary training, potential changes to business processes, and any disruptions that may occur during implementation.

5. Legal and Regulatory Feasibility: Projects must adhere to legal and regulatory requirements. This component ensures that the project complies with relevant laws, regulations, permits, and standards. Any legal hurdles or risks are identified and addressed during this phase.

6. Environmental and Social Feasibility: In today's world, the environmental and social impact of a project is crucial. This component evaluates the potential effects on the environment, local communities, and stakeholders. It considers sustainability,

ethical considerations, and the project's overall contribution to the greater good.

Steps in Conducting a Feasibility Study:

1. Project Definition: Clearly define the objectives, scope, and goals of the project. This provides a foundation for the study.

2. Data Collection and Analysis: Gather relevant data and information for each feasibility component. Conduct thorough research and analysis to understand the project's potential.

3. Assessment and Evaluation: Evaluate the collected data to determine the viability of the project. Compare the project's potential benefits against its risks and challenges.

4. Risk Identification and Mitigation: Identify potential risks and challenges that could affect project success. Develop strategies to mitigate or manage these risks.

5. Cost-Benefit Analysis: Compare the projected costs of the project against the anticipated benefits and returns. This analysis helps in determining if the project is financially feasible.

6. Recommendation: Based on the analysis, make a recommendation whether to proceed with the project, modify it, or abandon it altogether.

7. Report Presentation: Compile the findings, analysis, and recommendations into a comprehensive feasibility study report. Present the report to stakeholders, decision-makers, and

investors.

Conducting a feasibility study is an essential step in responsible project planning. It helps organizations make informed decisions, allocate resources effectively, and avoid potential pitfalls. A thorough feasibility study contributes to better project outcomes and minimizes the likelihood of costly failures.

3.1 Analyzing the Financial Viability of Your Business Idea

One of the most critical aspects of conducting a feasibility study is analyzing the financial viability of your business idea. This involves evaluating the potential costs and revenues associated with your proposed venture.

To begin you need to estimate the initial investment required to start your business. This may include costs such as purchasing equipment acquiring licenses and permits building or leasing a workspace hiring employees and other related expenses. It is crucial to conduct thorough research to obtain accurate and realistic cost estimates.

Next you should consider the projected revenue and sales potential of your business. This involves evaluating the demand for your product or service analyzing the target market and estimating the sales volume and pricing. You can conduct market research industry analysis and competitive analysis to gather relevant data and make informed projections.

Once you have estimated the initial investment and projected revenues you should calculate the expected costs and expenses associated with running your business. This includes costs like raw materials operational expenses marketing and advertising salaries utilities and any other ongoing expenses. It is important to be as comprehensive as possible when listing out the costs to have a clear understanding of the financial requirements.

To assess the financial viability of your business idea you need to calculate key financial metrics such as the return on investment (ROI break-even point and payback period. These metrics provide insights into the profitability and sustainability of your business.

ROI measures the profitability of an investment by comparing the gains or losses relative to the invested capital. It is calculated by deducting the total investment from the total profits and dividing it by the total investment. A higher ROI indicates a more financially viable business.

The break-even point is the level of sales at which your business neither makes a profit nor incurs a loss. It is calculated by dividing the total fixed costs by the contribution margin per unit which is the price per unit minus the variable cost per unit. The break-even point helps determine how much sales volume is needed to cover your costs and start making a profit.

The payback period reflects how long it takes for the initial investment to be recouped. It is calculated by dividing the initial investment by the annual net cash inflow. A shorter payback period implies a quicker return on investment.

By conducting a thorough financial analysis you can determine if your business idea is financially feasible. If the projected financials show positive indicators such as a high ROI a reasonable break-even point and a relatively short payback period it suggests a higher chance of success. On the other hand if the financial analysis reveals low profitability a prolonged break-even point or an extended payback period it may indicate potential risks and challenges.

3.2 Identifying Potential Risks and Challenges

Identifying potential risks and challenges is an essential part of a feasibility study. It helps you anticipate and mitigate issues that may arise during the implementation and operation of your business idea. Addressing potential risks early on can improve the chances of success and reduce potential losses.

There are several types of risks to consider including financial risks operational risks market risks legal and regulatory risks and competitive risks.

Financial risks involve factors that can impact the financial stability of your business. Examples include insufficient funding inaccurate financial projections high fixed costs and fluctuations in costs or revenues. By identifying these risks you can develop strategies to secure adequate funding revise financial projections and create contingency plans to handle unexpected fluctuations.

Operational risks pertain to the day-to-day operations of your business. They include issues like supply chain disruptions equipment breakdowns human resource challenges and production inefficiencies. By recognizing these risks you can implement measures to improve operational efficiency develop backup plans for potential disruptions and ensure you have the necessary resources and skills to address operational challenges.

Market risks involve factors that can affect the demand for your product or service. This includes changing consumer preferences emergence of new competitors shifts in market trends and economic downturns. Conducting market research staying informed about industry developments and periodically reassessing your target market can help you proactively respond to these risks.

Legal and regulatory risks are associated with compliance issues. Depending on the nature of your business you may need to comply with various local state or federal regulations and obtain necessary licenses and permits. Failure to comply with these requirements can result in fines legal actions or even the shutdown of your business. Therefore it is essential to identify and adhere to the relevant legal and regulatory obligations.

Competitive risks arise from competition within your industry. These risks include entering a saturated market facing aggressive competitors or being unable to differentiate your product or service from others. Identifying potential competitors understanding their strengths and weaknesses and developing unique selling points can help you mitigate these risks.

By identifying and assessing potential risks and challenges you can develop strategies and contingency plans to address them effectively. This enables you to make informed decisions and increases the likelihood of a successful business venture.

3.3 Developing a Business Plan

Developing a comprehensive business plan is an integral component of conducting a feasibility study. A business plan provides a roadmap for your venture outlining your goals strategies financial projections and operational plans.

A well-defined business plan typically includes the following sections:

1. Executive Summary: This section provides a concise overview of your business idea highlighting its key features target market competitive advantage and financial projections. It serves as an introduction to your business plan capturing the interest of potential investors or stakeholders.

2. Company Description: Here you provide background information about your company including its legal structure ownership mission statement and a summary of your products or services. This section gives readers a clear understanding of the nature of your business.

3. Market Analysis: In this section you conduct a detailed analysis of your target market industry trends customer demographics and competitive landscape. It demonstrates that you have thoroughly researched your market and possess a deep understanding of your target customers and industry dynamics.

4. Products or Services: This section provides a detailed description of your offerings. It explains their features benefits unique selling propositions pricing and any intellectual property rights associated with your products or services. This section helps investors and stakeholders understand the value proposition of your offerings.

5. Marketing and Sales Strategies: Here you outline your marketing and sales plans including distribution channels promotional activities pricing strategies and customer acquisition strategies. This section demonstrates how you plan to reach and attract your target customers.

6. Organization and Management: In this section you describe the organizational structure of your business and the roles and responsibilities of key personnel. This includes information about the management team's qualifications and relevant experience highlighting their capabilities to drive the success of the venture.

7. Financial Projections: This section presents detailed financial forecasts including projected income statements balance sheets and cash flow statements. It demonstrates the financial feasibility of your business by showcasing anticipated revenues expenses profitability and key financial ratios. Additionally it may include assumptions made during the forecasting process.

8. Funding Request: If you require external funding this section outlines your funding needs and the purpose of the funds. It includes information about your current financial position the amount of funding required and how the funds will be

utilized. Providing this information helps investors and lenders understand the financial requirements of your business.

9. Risk Assessment and Management: This section highlights the potential risks and challenges identified during the feasibility study and outlines strategies to mitigate them. It demonstrates your proactive approach to risk management and your ability to adapt to changing circumstances.

10. Implementation Plan: This section outlines the steps and timelines for implementing your business idea. It serves as a detailed roadmap guiding the execution of your plans and ensuring smooth implementation.

Developing a comprehensive business plan requires careful consideration and research. It should be tailored to your specific business idea industry and target market. A well-crafted and realistic business plan not only assists in decision-making but also serves as a tool for attracting investors securing financing and guiding the growth and development of your business.

In conclusion conducting a feasibility study involves analyzing the financial viability of your business idea identifying potential risks and challenges and developing a comprehensive business plan. By evaluating the financial aspects of your venture you can determine its profitability and sustainability. Identifying risks and challenges enables you to proactively address and mitigate issues that could impact the success of your business. And finally developing a comprehensive business plan provides a roadmap for executing your plans attracting investors and guiding your business's growth. With a thorough feasibility study you can make informed decisions and increase your chances of creating a successful and sustainable business.

Setting up Your Home-based Business

Setting up Your Home-based Business: Navigating the Essentials

Setting up a home-based business can offer flexibility, reduced overhead costs, and the convenience of working from the comfort of your own space. However, like any business venture, it requires careful planning and execution. Here's a brief explanation of the key steps involved in setting up your home-based business:

1. Idea and Niche Selection:
   Identify a business idea or niche that aligns with your skills, passions, and market demand. Research the market to ensure there's a viable customer base for your products or services.

2. Business Plan:
   Create a comprehensive business plan outlining your business goals, target audience, marketing strategy, competition analysis, and financial projections. A well-structured plan serves as a roadmap for your business's growth and success.

3. Legal Structure and Permits:

Choose a suitable legal structure for your business, such as sole proprietorship, LLC, or corporation. Register your business name and obtain any required licenses or permits, depending on your location and industry.

4. Home Office Setup:

Designate a dedicated workspace in your home that is comfortable, organized, and free from distractions. Ensure you have the necessary equipment, such as a computer, phone, and office supplies, to run your business efficiently.

5. Branding and Online Presence:

Develop a strong brand identity, including a memorable business name, logo, and consistent visual elements. Create a professional website and establish a presence on social media platforms relevant to your industry.

6. Financial Management:

Set up a separate business bank account to manage your finances. Implement bookkeeping and accounting practices to track income, expenses, and taxes accurately.

7. Marketing and Promotion:

Craft a marketing strategy to reach your target audience. Utilize online and offline marketing techniques, such as social media marketing, content creation, email campaigns, and networking events.

8. Product or Service Development:

If applicable, develop your products or services to meet customer needs and quality standards. Test and refine them before launching to ensure customer satisfaction.

9. Legal and Compliance:
   Understand your legal obligations, including tax regulations, data protection, and any industry-specific compliance requirements. Stay informed and compliant to avoid potential legal issues.

10. Time Management and Work-Life Balance:
   Establish a clear work schedule to maintain productivity and prevent burnout. Set boundaries between work and personal life to achieve a healthy work-life balance.

11. Customer Service and Relationship Building:
   Prioritize exceptional customer service to build positive relationships with your clients. Good customer experiences can lead to repeat business and referrals.

12. Continuous Learning and Adaptation:
   Stay updated with industry trends and continuously seek opportunities for improvement. Be open to adapting your business strategies based on feedback and changing market conditions.

Setting up a home-based business requires careful consideration of various aspects, from legal requirements to branding and customer service. With proper planning and dedication, a well-executed home-based business can provide you with both personal satisfaction and professional success.

4.1 Creating a Dedicated Workspace:

When setting up a home-based business it's important to establish a dedicated workspace that helps you maintain focus and separate your work life from your personal life. Here are some key steps to consider:

- Choose a designated area: Select a specific room or area in your home that will be dedicated solely to your business activities. Ideally this should be a quiet and secluded space where you can work without distractions.

- Arrange furniture and equipment: Set up your desk chair and any necessary equipment in a way that maximizes your productivity and comfort. Consider factors like good lighting proper ergonomics and ample storage space for your files and supplies.

- Create a professional atmosphere: Decorate your workspace in a way that reflects your business and creates a professional atmosphere. This can include organizing your books and materials hanging artwork or motivational posters and ensuring your surroundings are tidy and well-maintained.

4.2 Obtaining the Necessary Permits and Licenses:

Before starting your home-based business it's essential to research and obtain any required permits and licenses. The specific permits and licenses you need will vary based on your location and the type of business you operate. Here are some common steps to follow:

- Research local regulations: Contact your local government

or regulatory agencies to determine the specific permits and licenses required for your type of business. They can provide information on zoning regulations health and safety requirements and any other legal obligations.

- Obtain a business license: In many jurisdictions you will need to obtain a business license or permit to legally operate. This license ensures that you comply with local laws and regulations and may require you to pay a fee.

- Consider additional permits: Depending on your business activities you may need to obtain additional permits such as health department permits for food-related businesses building permits for home renovations or permits for signage and advertisement.

4.3 Setting Up Essential Equipment and Supplies:
   To effectively run your home-based business you'll need to equip your workspace with the necessary tools and supplies. Consider the following steps:

- Identify essential equipment: Determine the specific equipment you'll need to carry out your business activities. This could include computers printers scanners specialized software communication devices and any industry-specific machinery or tools.

- Purchase or lease equipment: Once you've identified your equipment needs research and acquire the necessary equipment. Depending on your budget you can choose to buy new or used equipment or opt for leasing options if available.

- Stock up on supplies: Identify the supplies and materials required for your business operations. This can include stationery printer ink packaging materials office supplies inventory and any other consumables related to your specific business.

- Establish inventory management: If your business involves selling products set up a system to manage your inventory effectively. This can include organizing storage space implementing inventory tracking tools or software and establishing a reorder system to ensure you have adequate stock levels.

Remember that these are general guidelines and it's important to research and comply with the legal and regulatory requirements specific to your location and business type. Consulting with legal and business professionals can also provide valuable insights and ensure you're setting up your home-based business correctly.

Building a Strong Online Presence

In today's digital age having a strong online presence is crucial for the success and growth of businesses. With more and more consumers turning to the internet to search for products and services it is essential for businesses to establish themselves online and effectively engage with their target audience. In this article we will explore three key strategies for building a strong online presence: creating a professional website implementing effective online marketing strategies and utilizing social media platforms for business growth.

5.1 Creating a Professional Website

A professional website serves as the online face of a business and is often the first point of contact for potential customers. It is essential to create a website that is visually appealing user-friendly and informative. Here are some key elements to consider when building a professional website:

1. Clear and Engaging Design: The design of a website should reflect the brand's identity and provide a positive user experience. Clear navigation aesthetically pleasing visuals and consistent branding elements should be incorporated into the website

design.

2. Responsive and Mobile-Friendly: With the increasing use of mobile devices it is imperative to ensure that the website is responsive and adjusts seamlessly to different screen sizes. A mobile-friendly website will enhance user experience and improve search engine rankings.

3. Well-Structured Content: The content on the website should be organized in a logical and intuitive manner. It should be easy for visitors to find the information they are looking for such as product descriptions contact details and relevant company information.

4. Search Engine Optimization (SEO): Implementing SEO techniques will help improve the visibility of the website in search engine results. This includes optimizing keywords meta tags and headings as well as creating high-quality content that aligns with relevant search queries.

5. User-friendly Conversion Elements: Incorporating clear call-to-action buttons contact forms and other conversion elements will help guide visitors towards desired actions such as making a purchase requesting a quote or signing up for a newsletter.

Example: A local bakery creates a professional website that showcases their delicious baked goods with high-resolution images and enticing descriptions. The website is mobile-friendly and includes a user-friendly navigation menu that allows visitors to easily find information about their products location and contact details. They also incorporate SEO techniques optimizing their website for keywords such as "local bakery" and "freshly baked bread which helps them rank higher in search engine results and attract more customers.

5.2 Implementing Effective Online Marketing Strategies

Once a professional website is created it is important to drive traffic to the site and convert visitors into customers. Implementing effective online marketing strategies can help businesses reach their target audience and promote their products or services. Here are some key online marketing strategies to consider:

1. Content Marketing: Creating and sharing valuable and informative content such as blog posts articles infographics and videos can help establish a business as an industry expert and attract potential customers. Content should be optimized for relevant keywords and shared on various platforms including the website social media and other relevant industry websites.

2. Search Engine Marketing (SEM): Utilizing paid advertising platforms such as Google Ads or Bing Ads allows businesses to display targeted ads to users who are actively searching for related products or services. SEM can help increase brand visibility drive traffic to the website and generate leads.

3. Email Marketing: Building an email list and sending regular newsletters or promotional emails can help keep customers engaged drive repeat business and generate leads. Personalized and targeted emails can be highly effective in nurturing relationships with customers.

4. Influencer Marketing: Collaborating with influencers or industry experts who have a strong online presence and following can help businesses reach a wider audience and build trust with potential customers. Influencers can promote products or services through sponsored content or product reviews.

Example: A fitness equipment company implements effective online marketing strategies by creating a blog on their website that provides valuable content about fitness tips workout routines and nutrition advice. They also optimize their website for SEO focusing on keywords such as "home gym equipment" and "best exercise machines." Through SEM they run targeted ads that appear when users search for fitness equipment or related terms. They build an email list by offering a free fitness e-book in exchange for visitors' email addresses and then send regular newsletters with exclusive discounts workout plans and product updates. In addition they collaborate with fitness influencers who promote their products on social media showcasing the benefits and features of their equipment to their followers.

5.3 Utilizing Social Media Platforms for Business Growth

Social media platforms have become integral to modern-day marketing strategies due to their vast reach engagement potential and ability to connect businesses directly with their customers. Leveraging social media effectively can help businesses build brand awareness engage with their audience and drive traffic to their website. Here are some key ways to utilize social media for business growth:

1. Consistent Branding: Ensuring consistent branding across all

social media platforms helps establish recognition and reinforce brand identity. This includes using the same logo color scheme and tone of voice to create a cohesive and memorable brand image.

2. Content Creation and Sharing: Creating and sharing high-quality content such as visuals videos blog posts and infographics relevant to the target audience can help attract and engage followers. Content should be tailored to each platform and encourage social sharing to expand the reach.

3. Customer Engagement: Actively engaging with customers through social media platforms helps build relationships gain valuable feedback and address customer queries or concerns. Responding promptly and genuinely to comments messages and reviews demonstrates excellent customer service.

4. Influencer Collaboration: Partnering with social media influencers who align with the brand's values and target audience can significantly increase the reach and credibility of a business. Influencers can promote products or services create sponsored content or feature the brand in their posts.

5. Paid Advertising: Many social media platforms offer paid advertising options such as Facebook Ads or Instagram Ads that allow businesses to target specific demographics and increase brand visibility. Paid advertising can be highly effective in reaching a larger audience and driving traffic to the website.

Example: A fashion brand utilizes social media platforms for business growth by consistently sharing visually appealing content that showcases their latest collections fashion tips and behind-the-scenes stories. They engage with their audience by responding to comments addressing customer queries and running interactive contests or giveaways. They collaborate with fashion influencers who post photos or videos featuring their clothing tagging the brand and giving a positive review. The brand also runs paid advertising campaigns on Instagram and Facebook targeting users who match their ideal customer profile based on interests demographics and behavior.

In conclusion building a strong online presence is essential for businesses to succeed in today's digital landscape. Creating a professional website implementing effective online marketing strategies and utilizing social media platforms are three key strategies that can help businesses establish visibility engage with the target audience and drive growth. By focusing on these strategies and continuously adapting to the evolving digital landscape businesses can thrive online and stay competitive in their respective industries.

Financial Management and Record Keeping

Financial management and record keeping are integral components of running a successful business, regardless of its size or nature. They provide a clear understanding of your business's financial health, facilitate informed decision-making, and ensure compliance with legal and tax obligations. Here's why these aspects are crucial:

1. Financial Visibility and Control:
   Effective financial management provides you with a clear view of your business's financial performance. It helps you monitor cash flow, track revenue and expenses, and identify trends. With this visibility, you can make timely adjustments and allocate resources strategically.

2. Budgeting and Planning:
   Maintaining accurate financial records allows you to create realistic budgets and financial forecasts. These tools help you plan for future expenses, investments, and growth initiatives. By setting financial goals and tracking progress, you can work towards achieving your business objectives.

3. Informed Decision-Making:

Access to up-to-date financial information empowers you to make informed decisions. Whether it's assessing the viability of a new project, determining pricing strategies, or evaluating cost-saving measures, well-managed financial records provide the data you need to make the right choices.

4. Tax Compliance:

Proper financial record keeping ensures that you accurately calculate and report your taxes. By maintaining organized records of income, expenses, deductions, and other financial transactions, you can meet your tax obligations and reduce the risk of audits or penalties.

5. Investor and Lender Confidence:

Investors and lenders often require transparent and well-documented financial records before considering investments or extending credit. Demonstrating strong financial management enhances your credibility and increases the likelihood of securing funding.

6. Business Performance Evaluation:

Financial records serve as a foundation for assessing your business's performance over time. You can analyze financial ratios, profitability, and other key metrics to identify areas of strength and areas that need improvement.

7. Legal Compliance:

Accurate financial record keeping ensures compliance with laws and regulations related to financial reporting and transparency. This is crucial for maintaining your business's reputation and avoiding legal issues.

8. Growth and Expansion:

When seeking opportunities for growth and expansion, clear financial records provide essential information for investors and stakeholders. They can evaluate your business's financial stability and potential for success.

9. Risk Management:

Effective financial management helps you identify and mitigate potential financial risks. By analyzing historical data and trends, you can anticipate challenges and develop strategies to overcome them.

10. Benchmarking and Comparison:

Well-maintained financial records allow you to benchmark your business's performance against industry standards and competitors. This helps you identify areas where you excel and areas where you might need improvement.

11. Succession Planning and Exit Strategies:

If you plan to pass on your business or sell it in the future, accurate financial records are essential for demonstrating the business's value and potential to prospective buyers or successors.

12. Accountability and Transparency:

Maintaining transparent financial records fosters a culture of accountability within your organization. Employees, partners, and stakeholders can trust that financial transactions are properly documented and reported.

In essence, financial management and record keeping provide the foundation for sound business operations, growth, and sustainability. By maintaining organized and accurate financial records, you empower your business to thrive, adapt to changing circumstances, and make informed strategic decisions.

6.1 Establishing a Separate Business Bank Account:

One of the fundamental aspects of financial management and record-keeping for any business is to establish a separate business bank account. This practice is crucial regardless of the size or type of business as it helps to separate personal and business finances. Here are a few reasons why establishing a separate business bank account is essential:

1. Legal and Compliance: Separating personal and business finances is not just best practice but in many jurisdictions a legal requirement for companies. Commingling personal and business funds can complicate financial reporting tax filings and legal liabilities. By maintaining a separate business bank account you can ensure compliance with legal and accounting regulations.

2. Financial Clarity: Having a separate bank account helps in achieving financial clarity. It allows you to accurately track your business income and expenses monitor cash flow and assess your financial health. This clarity is vital for making informed decisions and measuring the success of your business.

3. Professionalism: A separate business bank account reflects

professionalism and credibility. It provides a clear distinction between personal and business transactions giving the impression that your business is well-organized and serious. This can positively impact your relationships with vendors suppliers and clients.

4. Facilitates Accounting: By keeping personal and business finances separate you simplify your accounting processes. It eliminates the need to sift through personal transactions to identify business-related expenditures or income. When it comes time to prepare financial statements tax filings or apply for loans having a well-organized and accurate record becomes much more straightforward.

Example:

Let's consider an example of a small graphic design business owned by Sarah. Initially Sarah used her personal bank account to receive payments from clients and pay for business-related expenses. Over time this became increasingly complex as the number of transactions grew.

To streamline her financial management Sarah decided to open a separate business bank account. She visited her bank provided the necessary documentation and successfully established a dedicated account for her business. Now Sarah can track income manage expenses and perform accounting tasks with ease. The separation of funds also helps her prepare accurate financial statements and tax returns when needed.

6.2 Tracking Income and Expenses:

Tracking income and expenses is a vital aspect of financial management that all businesses should prioritize. By doing so businesses can gain a clear understanding of their revenue sources cost structure and profitability. Here are a few key reasons why tracking income and expenses is crucial:

1. Budgeting and Financial Planning: By tracking income and expenses businesses can create budgets and financial plans. Doing so allows you to set realistic revenue and expense targets allocate resources effectively and make informed decisions. This enables you to anticipate financial challenges and adjust your business strategy accordingly.

2. Cash Flow Management: Tracking income and expenses helps businesses maintain a healthy cash flow. You can accurately forecast cash inflows and outflows ensuring that you have sufficient funds to cover expenses pay employees invest in growth initiatives and meet financial obligations on time. The ability to manage cash flow effectively is crucial for businesses of all sizes.

3. Identifying Profitability: The tracking of income and expenses allows businesses to determine their profitability. By comparing revenue against expenses you can calculate the net income or loss your business is generating. This information helps you evaluate the financial viability of your operations and make necessary adjustments to improve profitability.

4. Tax Compliance: Tracking income and expenses is essential for tax compliance. By keeping records of all transactions you can accurately report income and claim deductions. This

ensures that you avoid penalties and interest charges resulting from incorrect or incomplete tax filings. It also helps during tax audits by providing supporting documentation for your financial activities.

Example:

Let's continue with Sarah's graphic design business. After opening her dedicated business bank account Sarah starts diligently tracking her income and expenses. She records all income received from her clients including the details of each project and payment received date. Additionally she maintains a record of all expenses related to her business such as software subscriptions office supplies and marketing costs.

Every month Sarah reviews her income and expenses to calculate her net income. This information helps her assess the profitability of her business and make informed decisions about future investments or cost-saving measures. Moreover when it's time to prepare tax returns Sarah can easily provide accurate income and expense details ensuring compliance with tax regulations.

6.3 Understanding Tax Obligations and Deductions:

Understanding tax obligations and deductions is crucial for effective financial management. Businesses are required to fulfill various tax obligations based on their jurisdiction industry and legal structure. Additionally taking advantage of eligible tax deductions can help reduce the tax burden and maximize business profitability. Here are a few key points to consider:

1. Tax Obligations: Every business is subject to specific tax obligations such as income tax sales tax payroll tax and property tax among others. It is essential to understand your tax requirements and comply with applicable laws and regulations. Failure to do so can result in penalties fines and legal issues. Consulting with a qualified tax professional is advisable to ensure proper compliance.

2. Accurate Record-Keeping: To meet tax obligations and claim deductions accurate record-keeping is critical. Maintain organized and detailed records of all financial transactions including sales expenses payroll and tax payments. These records serve as evidence during tax audits and enable you to report accurate information on tax returns.

3. Tax Deductions: Tax deductions can significantly reduce the taxable income of a business effectively reducing the tax liability. Common deductions include expenses related to business operations such as rent wages utilities travel and professional fees. Additionally there may be industry-specific tax incentives or credits that businesses can claim. It is essential to consult with a tax professional to identify and maximize eligible deductions.

4. Tax Planning: Effective tax planning can help optimize a business's tax position. By projecting income and expenses businesses can identify strategies to minimize taxes legally. This may involve strategies like deferring income or accelerating expenses. Tax planning should be an ongoing process considering changes in tax laws business circumstances and financial goals.

Example:

Sarah understands that she has specific tax obligations as a graphic design business owner. She reaches out to a tax professional to seek guidance on her tax obligations and possible deductions. The tax professional advises her on the applicable taxes deadlines and record-keeping requirements.

Based on her discussion with the tax professional Sarah learns that she can deduct business-related expenses such as software subscriptions marketing expenses office rent and professional fees. She ensures accurate record-keeping throughout the year maintaining receipts and invoices to support her tax deductions.

During tax season Sarah works with her tax professional to gather all the necessary information and documents required to file her tax return accurately. By understanding her tax obligations and making use of eligible deductions Sarah can optimize her tax position reduce her tax liability and ensure compliance with tax regulations.

In conclusion financial management and record-keeping are critical aspects of running a business successfully. By establishing a separate business bank account tracking income and expenses and understanding tax obligations and deductions businesses can ensure financial transparency comply with legal requirements make informed decisions and maximize profitability. It is essential to maintain accurate records seek professional advice when needed and regularly review and adapt financial practices to suit changing business needs.

Finding Customers and Generating Sales

To ensure business success it is crucial to identify your target audience and implement effective marketing strategies to attract and engage potential customers. Additionally leveraging networking opportunities and collaborations can further enhance your customer base and generate sales. Let's explore each of these aspects in more detail with examples.

7.1 Identifying Your Target Audience:

Identifying your target audience involves understanding the characteristics and preferences of the individuals or businesses most likely to buy your product or service. By focusing your marketing efforts on a specific group you can tailor your messaging and create a more compelling value proposition. Here are a few examples:

a) B2C Example: A company that sells athletic shoes might identify their target audience as young adults who are active and value stylish footwear. By targeting this group specifically through social media ads and influencers they can create compelling content and offers that resonate with their audience's interests.

b) B2B Example: A software development company may identify their target audience as small to medium-sized businesses who need customized software solutions. They can then create targeted email campaigns and attend industry-specific events or trade shows to connect with potential clients and showcase their expertise.

7.2 Implementing Effective Marketing and Advertising Strategies:

Marketing and advertising strategies are essential for finding customers and driving sales. By utilizing various platforms and techniques businesses can increase their visibility and reach their target audience. Some examples include:

a) Content Marketing: Creating valuable and relevant content such as blog posts videos or podcasts that educates and engages potential customers. This strategy builds trust and positions your business as an industry expert.

b) Social Media Advertising: Utilizing social media platforms like Facebook Instagram or LinkedIn to run targeted advertisements. These platforms offer precise targeting options to reach specific demographics interests or geographic locations.

c) Search Engine Optimization (SEO): Optimizing your website and content to rank higher in search engine results. This strategy improves visibility when potential customers search for relevant keywords driving organic traffic to your website.

7.3 Leveraging Networking Opportunities and Collaborations:

Networking and collaborations provide opportunities to establish valuable connections and expand your customer base. Here are a few examples:

a) Attending Industry Events: Participating in conferences seminars or trade shows related to your industry allows you to meet potential customers and business partners. It provides an avenue for showcasing your products or services and building relationships.

b) partnering with Complementary Businesses: Collaborating with businesses that offer complementary products or services can help you reach new customers. For example a wedding planner may collaborate with a photographer a florist and a venue to offer bundled services attracting a broader customer base.

c) Influencer Partnerships: Partnering with influencers or industry experts who have a significant online following can help increase brand visibility and attract new customers. For instance a health supplement brand may collaborate with fitness influencers to promote their products to their audience.

In summary finding customers and generating sales involves identifying your target audience implementing effective marketing strategies and leveraging networking opportunities and collaborations. By understanding your audience's needs engaging them through tailored marketing campaigns and building meaningful connections you can increase your customer base and drive sales for your business.

Balancing Work and Personal Life

Navigating Priorities

Balancing work and personal life involves effectively managing your professional responsibilities and personal well-being. It's about finding harmony between your career aspirations and spending quality time with loved ones and pursuing personal interests. Achieving this balance is essential for overall satisfaction and preventing burnout. Here's a brief explanation:

1. Prioritization: Balancing work and personal life requires prioritizing tasks and activities based on their importance and impact. This ensures that you allocate time and energy to both work-related responsibilities and personal activities.

2. Time Management: Efficiently managing your time helps you achieve your work goals while also having time for relaxation, hobbies, and spending time with family and friends.

3. Boundaries: Set clear boundaries between work and personal time. Avoid bringing work-related stress into your personal space and vice versa. This separation enhances your ability to fully engage in both domains.

4. Delegation: Delegate tasks at work and enlist the support of family members or hired help for personal responsibilities. Delegating enables you to focus on what truly matters in each aspect of your life.

5. Self-Care: Prioritize self-care to maintain physical, mental, and emotional well-being. Regular exercise, proper nutrition, and relaxation techniques contribute to your overall ability to handle both work and personal commitments.

6. Flexibility: Embrace flexibility in your schedule to accommodate unexpected events or opportunities. Having a certain level of flexibility reduces stress when juggling work and personal demands.

7. Communication: Openly communicate with your employer, colleagues, and family about your availability and commitments. Clear communication helps manage expectations and reduces misunderstandings.

8. Quality Over Quantity: Focus on the quality of time spent rather than the quantity. Being fully present during work hours and quality time with loved ones leads to more meaningful experiences.

9. Saying No: Learn to say no to additional work tasks or personal commitments when you're already stretched thin. Prioritize what aligns with your current goals and responsibilities.

10. Reflection: Regularly reflect on your priorities and assess whether your current balance aligns with your goals and values.

Adjustments may be necessary as circumstances change.

11. Technology Boundaries: Limit the use of technology during personal time to avoid distractions and maintain a healthy work-life separation.

12. Adaptability: Recognize that achieving a perfect balance is a continuous journey. Circumstances change, and adapting your approach allows you to navigate new challenges effectively.

Balancing work and personal life is a dynamic endeavor that requires ongoing adjustments and self-awareness. Striving for equilibrium enhances your overall happiness, well-being, and ability to thrive in both your professional and personal spheres.

Part 1: Setting Boundaries and Establishing a Schedule

Balancing work and personal life requires setting boundaries and establishing a schedule that allows you to dedicate time and energy to both spheres. Without proper boundaries it can be challenging to find a healthy balance between your work commitments and personal priorities. Here are some strategies to help you set boundaries and establish a schedule:

1. Clearly define your work hours: Determine the specific hours during which you are available for work-related tasks. Communicate these hours to your colleagues and clients to manage their expectations and minimize interruptions during your personal time. For example you may decide that your workday starts at 9:00 am and ends at 5:00 pm.

2. Create a designated workspace: Set up a dedicated area for

work within your home or office. This physical separation can signal the start and end of your workday and help maintain a clear boundary between work and personal life. When you leave this space it becomes easier to mentally shift your focus to personal matters.

3. Limit out-of-work communication: Establish guidelines for communicating outside of work hours. It is crucial to agree on reasonable response times with your colleagues or clients to avoid feeling constantly on call. For instance you may choose to respond to urgent messages within a specific time frame while leaving non-urgent matters for the next workday.

4. Utilize technology tools: Take advantage of technology tools that enable you to automate and streamline tasks such as email filters and scheduling software. These tools can help you prioritize your workload reduce time spent on administrative tasks and create more efficient workflows.

5. Set boundaries with your loved ones: Communicate your work commitments with your family and friends ensuring they understand the constraints and demands of your profession. This open communication will help foster understanding and support allowing you to focus on your work when needed while still maintaining personal connections.

Part 2: Managing Time Effectively

Managing your time effectively is essential for achieving a balance between work and personal life. When you prioritize and use your time efficiently you can accomplish your professional tasks while still allocating quality time to personal endeavors. Consider the following time management strategies:

1. Prioritize tasks: Prioritization is crucial for managing your time effectively. Identify the most important and urgent tasks and give them your immediate attention. This approach helps prevent procrastination and ensures that essential work is completed on time.

2. Create a to-do list: Develop a daily or weekly to-do list that outlines your tasks and deadlines. By organizing your tasks in a list you can keep track of your progress and maintain a clear overview of what needs to be accomplished. Prioritize your tasks on this list to stay focused and avoid feeling overwhelmed.

3. Delegate and outsource: Recognize when certain tasks can be delegated or outsourced to others. Delegating responsibilities to colleagues or outsourcing to external professionals can help you free up time for more critical tasks or personal activities.

4. Avoid multitasking: While it may seem productive to juggle multiple tasks simultaneously it often leads to reduced efficiency and decreased focus. Instead focus on one task at a time complete it and then move on to the next. This approach allows you to give proper attention to each task resulting in higher quality outcomes.

5. Incorporate breaks and downtime: Allow for regular breaks throughout your workday to recharge and maintain concentration. Research has shown that taking short breaks can increase productivity and mental well-being. Additionally make sure to

schedule personal downtime to engage in activities that bring you joy and help you relax.

Part 3: Taking Care of Your Well-being

Maintaining a healthy work-life balance involves prioritizing your well-being. Neglecting self-care can lead to burnout and negatively impact both your professional performance and personal life. Here are some strategies to help you take care of your well-being:

1. Practice self-care activities: Engage in activities that promote your physical mental and emotional well-being. This can include regular exercise mindfulness or meditation practices spending time in nature pursuing hobbies or connecting with loved ones.

2. Set aside time for relaxation: Allocate specific periods for relaxation and rejuvenation. This can be in the form of scheduled breaks during work hours regular evenings or weekends dedicated to unwinding or taking vacations to recharge. Prioritize rest as an integral part of your routine.

3. Establish boundaries around personal time: Just as setting work boundaries is important it is equally vital to establish boundaries around personal time. Avoid bringing work-related stress into your personal life and resist the urge to constantly check emails or respond to work-related matters outside of designated work hours.

4. Seek support when needed: Don't hesitate to reach out for

support when you feel overwhelmed. Whether it's seeking advice from a mentor talking to a trusted colleague or seeking professional help having a support system in place can provide you with guidance and alleviate stress.

5. Regularly reassess and adjust: Recognize that finding a balance between work and personal life is an ongoing process. Regularly reassess your priorities schedules and boundaries to ensure they align with your current circumstances and goals. Flexibility and adaptability are key in maintaining balance over time.

Examples:

To better understand how these strategies can be implemented in real-life situations let's consider a few examples:

Example 1: Sarah is a marketing manager who often finds herself working late into the night and sacrificing her personal time. She decides to set boundaries and establish a schedule by clearly defining her work hours from 9:00 am to 5:00 pm. She communicates this to her team and clients ensuring they understand her availability. Sarah also creates a designated workspace in her home and avoids using that space for personal activities. By doing so she establishes a physical boundary between work and personal life.

Example 2: Mark a freelance graphic designer struggles with effective time management. He often feels overwhelmed by multiple projects and ends up working on several tasks simultaneously. To manage his time effectively Mark starts prioritizing tasks by creating a to-do list and assigning deadlines to each item. He focuses on one task at a time completing it before moving on to the next. This approach helps him stay organized increase his productivity and reduce stress.

Example 3: Lisa a software engineer realizes that she neglects her well-being by constantly working through her breaks and bringing work-related stress into her personal life. To take care of her well-being Lisa starts incorporating regular breaks into her workday. She uses these breaks to stretch meditate or engage in a quick relaxation exercise. Additionally she establishes strict boundaries around her personal time setting aside specific hours each day to pursue her hobbies and spend time with family and friends.

In conclusion balancing work and personal life requires setting boundaries managing time effectively and taking care of your well-being. By implementing these strategies and examples you can create a harmonious integration of both aspects leading to increased productivity satisfaction and overall well-being in your life. Remember finding the right balance is a continuous process that may require adjustments along the way. Take time to regularly assess and fine-tune your approach to maintain a healthy work-life balance.

Scaling Your Home-based Business

Scaling a home-based business involves expanding its operations while maintaining control over quality and customer satisfaction. It's a strategic approach to growing your venture beyond its initial scope. Here's a brief explanation:

1. Efficient Systems: Implement streamlined processes and systems to handle increased demand without compromising quality or efficiency.

2. Resource Management: Allocate resources wisely, considering factors like staffing, technology, and infrastructure, to support growth effectively.

3. Market Research: Understand market trends and customer preferences to identify opportunities for expansion and tailor your offerings.

4. Marketing Strategy: Develop a robust marketing plan to reach a broader audience and generate increased interest in your products or services.

5. Scalable Technology: Invest in technology that can accom-

modate higher volumes of sales, communication, and data management.

6. Financial Planning: Ensure your financial resources are sufficient to cover the costs of expansion and to sustain growth in the long term.

7. Quality Control: Maintain consistent quality standards as you grow, ensuring customer satisfaction remains a priority.

8. Team Building: If necessary, build a capable team to share responsibilities and contribute to the business's growth.

9. Customer Feedback: Listen to customer feedback to identify areas for improvement and address concerns promptly.

10. Flexibility: Adapt your strategies as your business scales, remaining agile in response to changing market dynamics.

Scaling your home-based business requires strategic decision-making to ensure sustainable growth and a positive impact on your bottom line.

9.1 Identifying Growth Opportunities

Scaling your home-based business requires careful identification of growth opportunities. You need to analyze your current market customer demand and competitive landscape to understand how you can expand your business.

Start by conducting market research to identify potential untapped markets or customer segments. Look for opportunities to offer new products or services or cater to a broader customer base. Consider if there is a demand for your offerings in different geographical regions or if there are complementary industries you can target.

Additionally explore diversification strategies to reduce dependence on a single market or product. For example you can consider expanding your product line reaching out to new customer segments or exploring related industries.

Collaborate with other entrepreneurs industry associations and local business networks to gain insights and identify potential growth opportunities. Attend industry conferences trade shows and networking events to connect with like-minded individuals and uncover new possibilities.

9.2 Hiring Employees or Outsourcing

As your home-based business scales you might need to hire employees or outsource certain tasks to manage the increased workload effectively. Determine which parts of your business require additional manpower or expertise and assess whether it makes more sense to recruit in-house or outsource to a third party.

Hiring employees allows you to have more direct control over your business operations. You can carefully select individuals whose skills align with your business needs and provide them with guidance and training. Keep in mind that hiring employees comes with additional responsibilities such as payroll taxes benefits and office space if needed.

Outsourcing on the other hand allows you to tap into specialized skills and expertise without the long-term commitments of hiring full-time employees. You can outsource tasks like accounting marketing customer service or manufacturing to external service providers freelancers or contractors. This can help reduce costs increase efficiency and focus on your core competencies.

Both hiring and outsourcing have their pros and cons so weigh your options based on your specific needs budget and growth plans.

9.3 Scaling Operations and Increasing Production

Scaling your home-based business often requires expanding your operations and increasing production capacity. This can involve various strategies such as streamlining processes investing in equipment or technology and optimizing your supply chain.

To streamline processes evaluate your current workflows and identify areas for improvement. Eliminate bottlenecks automate repetitive tasks and implement standardized procedures to increase efficiency. This can help reduce costs improve productivity and enable your business to handle larger volumes of work.

Investing in equipment machinery or technology can boost your production capabilities. Consider the specific needs of your business such as increased manufacturing capacity or improved communication systems and invest in the right resources. This might involve purchasing new equipment upgrading existing technology or implementing software solutions to optimize your operations.

Optimizing your supply chain is crucial for scaling operations. Look for ways to source materials or products more efficiently negotiate better contracts with suppliers and establish reliable partnerships. Implement inventory management systems to minimize stockouts and reduce lead times ensuring a smooth flow of goods or services to meet growing demand.

Regularly analyze and monitor the efficiency of your operations to identify areas for improvement. Keep track of key performance indicators (KPIs) such as production output quality control and turnaround times to ensure you're effectively scaling your operations.

9.4 Expanding Your Customer Base

Expanding your customer base is a critical aspect of scaling your home-based business. By reaching new customers you can increase your sales and revenue. Here are some strategies to consider:

1. Develop a comprehensive marketing plan: Identify your target audience and create a marketing strategy to reach them effectively. Utilize a mix of digital marketing techniques such as social media content marketing search engine optimization (SEO and paid advertising to expand your reach.

2. Enhance customer experience: Prioritize customer satisfaction and retention by providing excellent service and personalized experiences. Encourage customer referrals and positive online reviews to attract new customers.

3. Explore new sales channels: Consider selling through additional channels such as online marketplaces retail stores or partnering with distributors. Expand your reach geographically by targeting customers in new regions or countries.

4. Offer new products or services: Extend your product or service line to cater to a wider range of customer needs. Launching new offerings can attract new customers and encourage repeat business.

5. Leverage social proof: Showcase testimonials case studies and success stories to build credibility and trust with potential customers. Social proof can be a powerful tool in convincing new customers to choose your business.

Remember to continuously analyze your marketing efforts and gather customer feedback to refine your strategies and improve your targeting.

9.5 Improving Systems and Processes

As your home-based business scales it becomes essential to focus on improving systems and processes for increased efficiency and productivity. Here are some key areas to consider:

1. Standardize workflows: Establish standardized processes

for routine tasks to ensure consistency and eliminate errors. Document these processes and provide training to employees or contractors to ensure everyone follows the same procedures.

2. Implement project management tools: Use project management tools to track tasks deadlines and progress. This helps improve collaboration communication and overall efficiency within your team.

3. Embrace technology: Leverage technology and automation to streamline operations. Implement software solutions such as customer relationship management (CRM inventory management accounting or project management software to simplify repetitive tasks and save time.

4. Establish effective communication channels: Ensure effective communication within your team customers and suppliers. Use collaboration tools video conferencing or cloud-based platforms to ensure smooth communication and information sharing.

5. Continuously analyze and optimize: Regularly review your processes and systems to identify areas for improvement. Seek feedback from employees customers and partners to identify pain points or bottlenecks. Use data and analytics to track performance and make data-driven decisions.

By continuously improving systems and processes you can increase productivity reduce errors and enhance customer satisfaction.

9.6 Utilizing Technology and Automation

Technology and automation play a crucial role in scaling your home-based business. By leveraging the right tools and systems you can automate repetitive tasks improve efficiency and free up resources to focus on strategic activities. Here are some ways to utilize technology and automation effectively:

1. Customer Relationship Management (CRM) systems: Implement a CRM system to manage customer data track interactions and streamline sales and marketing processes. This allows you to effectively manage relationships with a growing customer base.

2. E-commerce platforms: If you sell products online consider utilizing e-commerce platforms that handle inventory management order processing and payment integration. This can significantly streamline your operations and enhance the customer buying experience.

3. Accounting and financial management systems: Implement software solutions for accounting bookkeeping and financial management. This helps automate financial processes track expenses and revenue and generate financial reports.

4. Social media management tools: Use social media management tools to schedule posts engage with followers and analyze performance across different platforms. This helps amplify your online presence and reach a wider audience.

5. Task management and collaboration tools: Utilize project

management or task management tools to effectively manage tasks deadlines and team collaboration. This improves communication and ensures everyone is aligned with project goals.

6. Chatbots and automated customer service: Integrate chatbots or automated customer service systems to handle routine customer inquiries and provide quick responses. This frees up your time and resources while still delivering a satisfactory customer experience.

Remember to assess your specific business needs and choose technology solutions that align with your goals and budget. Regularly review and update your technology stack as new tools and advancements become available.

9.7 Building Strategic Partnerships

Building strategic partnerships can be instrumental in scaling your home-based business. Strategic partnerships allow you to tap into the expertise resources and customer base of other businesses to accelerate growth. Consider the following when building strategic partnerships:

1. Identify complementary businesses: Look for businesses that offer products or services that complement yours. Partnerships with businesses that target the same customer base but have non-competing offerings can be mutually beneficial.

2. Networking events and industry associations: Attend networking events conferences or join industry associations where you can connect with potential partners. Engage in conversa-

tions share your vision and explore collaboration opportunities.

3. Joint marketing campaigns: Collaborate with partners on joint marketing campaigns to reach a broader audience. This could involve co-promoting each other's products or services sharing marketing collateral or hosting joint events.

4. Co-creating new offerings: Explore opportunities to co-create new products or services with partners. By combining your unique strengths and resources you can offer innovative solutions that cater to a wider customer base.

5. Sharing resources or distribution channels: Consider sharing resources facilities or distribution channels with strategic partners. This can help reduce costs increase efficiency and extend your reach.

Building strategic partnerships requires clear communication trust and a shared vision. Ensure partnerships are mutually beneficial and enhance the value proposition for both parties involved.

9.8 Managing Finances and Cash Flow

Managing finances and cash flow becomes increasingly crucial as your home-based business scales. Proper financial management ensures stability enables growth and minimizes risks. Consider the following practices to manage your finances effectively:

1. Budgeting and forecasting: Develop a budget and financial

forecast to track income expenses and projected cash flow. This helps you plan for growth and make informed financial decisions.

2. Separate business and personal finances: Establish separate bank accounts and credit cards for your business to maintain clarity and separation. This simplifies accounting tax filings and allows you to track business expenses accurately.

3. Regularly monitor cash flow: Keep a close eye on cash flow by regularly monitoring accounts receivable and payable. Ensure you have enough liquidity to cover expenses pay employees or contractors and invest in growth opportunities.

4. Invoice promptly and follow up on payments: Invoice customers promptly and establish clear payment terms. Follow up on overdue invoices to minimize cash flow gaps and maintain healthy working capital.

5. Implement a bookkeeping system: Establish proper book-keeping practices and systems to track income expenses and financial transactions. This enables accurate financial reporting tax preparation and compliance.

6. Monitor and control expenses: Regularly review your expenses to identify areas where you can reduce costs or improve efficiency. Negotiate with suppliers for better pricing and consider outsourcing non-core activities to reduce overhead.

7. Seek professional advice: Consult with a financial advisor or accountant to ensure you have a solid financial strategy in place.

They can offer guidance on tax planning risk management and investment opportunities.

Managing finances and cash flow requires discipline attention to detail and a proactive approach. Regularly review and assess your financial performance to make necessary adjustments and mitigate any potential risks.

9.9 Measuring and Monitoring Success

To effectively scale your home-based business it's crucial to measure and monitor your success. This allows you to track progress identify areas for improvement and make data-driven decisions. Consider the following approaches to measure and monitor your success:

1. Key performance indicators (KPIs): Establish key metrics that are relevant to your business objectives. These could include sales growth customer acquisition rate conversion rate customer satisfaction scores or average order value. Regularly track and analyze these metrics to gauge performance.

2. Data analysis and reporting: Utilize data analytics tools to gather insights from your business data. This can help identify patterns trends and opportunities. Generate regular reports to share with stakeholders and facilitate informed decision-making.

3. Customer feedback and reviews: Actively seek feedback from customers through surveys reviews or testimonials. Positive feedback can validate your efforts and help attract new cus-

tomers while negative feedback provides valuable insights for improvement.

4. Benchmarking: Compare your performance against industry benchmarks or competitors to understand your relative position. This can help you identify areas where you excel and areas that require improvement.

5. Regular performance reviews: Conduct regular performance reviews of your business and teams. Evaluate individual and team performance against set goals provide constructive feedback and align future objectives.

6. Continuous improvement: Cultivate a culture of continuous improvement within your organization. Encourage innovation explore new ideas and celebrate successes. Regularly revisit your strategies objectives and processes to ensure they align with your long-term vision.

By consistently measuring and monitoring your success you can identify areas that require attention make necessary adjustments and ensure sustainable growth.

9.10 Overcoming Challenges and Risks

Scaling your home-based business is not without its challenges and risks. However with careful planning and execution you can navigate through these obstacles. Consider the following strategies to overcome common challenges:

1. Manage growing pains: Scaling often comes with operational

challenges resource constraints and increased workload. Be prepared to adapt your operations workflows and systems to handle the increased demands. Hire qualified employees or outsource to alleviate overwhelm and ensure smooth operations.

2. Secure funding: Scaling may require additional capital to invest in infrastructure technology marketing or human resources. Explore funding options such as small business loans grants angel investors or crowdfunding platforms.

3. Maintain customer satisfaction: As your business grows it becomes crucial to maintain high levels of customer satisfaction. Focus on providing personalized experiences offering excellent customer support and ensuring consistent product or service quality.

4. Monitor competition: Keep an eye on your competitors and industry trends. Identify potential threats or disruptions and adapt your strategies accordingly. Stay agile and be willing to pivot when necessary.

5. Regulatory and compliance considerations: As your business expands it's essential to stay updated on relevant regulations licensing requirements and compliance standards. Consult legal or industry experts as needed to ensure your business remains compliant.

6. Scalability of operations: Consider scalability from the early stages of your business. Structure your processes systems and technology to support growth. This minimizes disruptions and allows for seamless scaling.

7. Stay focused and adaptable: Scaling requires a clear vision and focus. At the same time be adaptable and willing to make adjustments based on market shifts or customer demands. Continuously evaluate and iterate your strategies to maximize results.

Remember that challenges and risks are inherent to business growth. Approach them as opportunities for learning innovation and improvement. Seek guidance from mentors industry experts or colleagues who have successfully scaled their businesses.

9.11 Conclusion

Scaling your home-based business requires careful planning strategic decision-making and continuous adaptation. By identifying growth opportunities hiring employees or outsourcing scaling operations and increasing production expanding your customer base improving systems and processes utilizing technology and automation building strategic partnerships managing finances and cash flow and measuring and monitoring success you can effectively scale your business and achieve sustainable growth.

The path to scaling your home-based business may not always be smooth but perseverance resilience and strategic execution will pave the way for success. Embrace challenges learn from experiences and constantly innovate to maximize your business's growth potential.

Challenges and Solutions

Challenges and Solutions in Scaling Your Home-based Business

Challenges:

1. Resource Limitations: Limited funds, space, and manpower can hinder your business's ability to expand.

2. Maintaining Quality: Ensuring consistent quality as operations grow can be challenging.

3. Time Management: Balancing increased responsibilities and time demands can lead to burnout.

4. Customer Retention: Sustaining customer loyalty during expansion requires careful attention.

5. Operational Efficiency: Processes may become inefficient or strained with higher demand.

Solutions:

1. Strategic Investment: Secure funding or reinvest profits to

acquire necessary resources for expansion.

2. Standardization: Implement standardized procedures and quality control measures to maintain consistency.

3. Delegation: Delegate tasks to free up time for strategic decision-making and personal well-being.

4. Personalized Engagement: Prioritize customer relationships through personalized interactions and exceptional service.

5. Process Optimization: Continuously refine processes to ensure efficiency and minimize bottlenecks.

Successfully scaling your home-based business involves addressing these challenges with strategic solutions, allowing controlled growth while upholding quality and customer satisfaction.

Here's a further explanation of the challenges and solutions for overcoming isolation and staying motivated dealing with potential distractions and adapting to changing business needs:

10.1 Overcoming Isolation and Staying Motivated:

Remote work can be isolating especially when you don't have colleagues around you. The lack of social interaction and support can lead to decreased motivation and productivity. To overcome this challenge it's crucial to establish a routine and create a dedicated workspace that can help separate work from personal life.

You can also set regular virtual check-ins with your colleagues or managers to maintain communication and stay connected. Engaging in online communities or professional networks can provide a sense of belonging and support. Additionally taking regular breaks and incorporating exercise or other activities throughout the day can help combat isolation and keep you motivated.

10.2 Dealing with Potential Distractions:

Working from home can expose you to various distractions such as household activities family members or personal devices. These distractions can significantly impact your focus and productivity. Creating a designated workspace free from distractions can be helpful. Let your family or roommates know your working hours and request their cooperation to minimize interruptions.

Establishing a structured schedule can also assist in managing distractions. Prioritize tasks and establish deadlines to stay focused. Utilize productivity tools or time management techniques like the Pomodoro Technique which breaks work into manageable intervals alternating with short breaks.

Implementing effective digital organization and time-blocking techniques can help mitigate potential distractions and enhance your ability to stay on track.

10.3 Adapting to Changing Business Needs:

The nature of business is dynamic and remote work can further bring about changes in the way tasks are performed. To adapt to changing business needs it's essential to stay flexible and open to learning new skills or tools.

Regular communication with your team and managers is vital to ensure you are aware of any changes or updates in business requirements. It's crucial to maintain a growth mindset and be receptive to feedback and constructive criticism. This will allow you to adapt quickly and efficiently to the evolving needs of the business.

Proactively seeking professional development opportunities such as online courses or workshops can equip you with the necessary skills to handle changing demands. Embracing technology and utilizing collaboration tools can also enhance your ability to adapt and work effectively in a remote environment.

By staying adaptable open-minded and proactive you can successfully navigate changing business needs and continue to thrive in a remote work setting.

250 tips for starting a small business from home

1. Define your business idea and goals.

2. Conduct thorough market research.

3. Identify your target market and ideal customer profile.

4. Create a business plan outlining your strategies and objectives.

5. Establish a dedicated workspace in your home.

6. Set aside specific working hours to maintain a healthy work-life balance.

7. Create a professional business name and register it.

8. Obtain any necessary permits or licenses.

9. Set up a separate business bank account.

10. Clearly define your products or services and their unique selling points.

11. Invest in a professional website and optimize it for search engines.

12. Use social media platforms to promote your business.

13. Network with other small business owners for support and collaboration.

14. Develop a strong brand identity with a logo colors and consistent messaging.

15. Create business cards and other promotional materials.

16. Offer excellent customer service to build loyalty and drive repeat business.

17. Consider offering a free trial or introductory offer to attract new customers.

18. Monitor your competitors and analyze their marketing strategies.

19. Track your business expenses and keep thorough financial records.

20. Consider using accounting software to manage your finances.

21. Set pricing strategically to ensure profitability.

22. Offer multiple payment options for customer convenience.

23. Establish efficient supply chain management if applicable.

24. Continually update your product or service offerings to meet customer needs.

25. Stay on top of industry trends and changes.

26. Consider offering a subscription-based model for recurring revenue.

27. Utilize email marketing to nurture and engage with your customer base.

28. Seek feedback from customers to improve your products or services.

29. Develop a content marketing strategy to establish thought leadership.

30. Attend trade shows or industry conferences to network and gain exposure.

31. Leverage online advertising platforms such as Google Ads or Facebook Ads.

32. Offer referral incentives to encourage satisfied customers to recommend your business.

33. Establish partnerships with complementary businesses

for cross-promotion.

34. Consider offering add-on services or upsells to increase revenue.

35. Develop a strong online presence by participating in forums or online communities.

36. Consider offering a loyalty program to reward repeat customers.

37. Create compelling product descriptions and images for online listings.

38. Utilize search engine optimization techniques to improve your website''s visibility.

39. Engage with your audience through blog posts or video content.

40. Offer discounts or promotions during slow periods to boost sales.

41. Leverage social media influencers to reach a wider audience.

42. Attend local networking events to connect with potential customers.

43. Offer educational webinars or workshops to establish credibility.

44. Consider joining industry-specific associations or organizations.

45. Develop strategic partnerships with suppliers or distributors.

46. Systemize your business processes to increase efficiency.

47. Outsource tasks such as accounting or customer service if needed.

48. Offer personalized customer experiences to stand out from competitors.

49. Stay up to date with legal and regulatory requirements for

your industry.

50. Obtain appropriate insurance coverage to protect your business.

51. Continually educate yourself on business and industry best practices.

52. Consider joining a mastermind group for support and mentorship.

53. Utilize video marketing to showcase your products or services.

54. Offer free downloadable resources or guides to attract leads.

55. Leverage customer testimonials or reviews to build trust.

56. Implement a customer relationship management (CRM) system to track interactions.

57. Use data analytics to gain insights into customer behavior and preferences.

58. Consider offering a subscription box service if applicable to your industry.

59. Develop a strong personal brand to establish credibility.

60. Stay organized with project management tools and calendars.

61. Prioritize self-care to avoid burnout.

62. Continually innovate and adapt to changing market trends.

63. Consider offering customized or personalized products.

64. Attend local business workshops or seminars to enhance your skills.

65. Create video tutorials or guides to showcase your expertise.

66. Offer free samples or trials to attract new customers.

67. Leverage user-generated content by encouraging cus-

tomers to share experiences.

68. Invest in high-quality product packaging and shipping materials.

69. Develop a clear return or refund policy for customer satisfaction.

70. Utilize live chat or chatbot features on your website for customer support.

71. Offer limited-time promotions or flash sales to create urgency.

72. Participate in trade fairs or exhibitions to showcase your products.

73. Hire freelancers or virtual assistants for additional support.

74. Stay connected with industry news through newsletters or subscriptions.

75. Utilize online marketplaces to reach a wider audience.

76. Offer bundled products or services for increased value.

77. Develop a strong customer onboarding process to ensure satisfaction.

78. Use explainer videos to showcase product features and benefits.

79. Host webinars or online workshops to engage with potential customers.

80. Give back to the community by partnering with local charities or causes.

81. Offer a referral program with incentives for existing customers.

82. Utilize email automation to nurture leads and follow up with customers.

83. Develop an affiliate marketing program to expand your reach.

84. Create an email newsletter to stay connected with customers.

85. Offer discounts or exclusive offers to email subscribers.

86. Optimize your website for mobile devices for a seamless user experience.

87. Collaborate with influencers or bloggers for sponsored content.

88. Create engaging social media content such as polls or quizzes.

89. Utilize user-generated hashtags to encourage customers to share their experiences.

90. Develop a customer loyalty program with tiers or rewards.

91. Create online tutorial videos to educate customers about your products.

92. Offer free resources or templates related to your industry.

93. Collaborate with other small businesses for marketing campaigns.

94. Offer limited editions or exclusive products to create buzz.

95. Develop partnerships with local businesses for cross-promotion.

96. Offer free consultations or demos to attract new clients.

97. Develop a strategic pricing structure for your services.

98. Optimize your website loading speed for improved user experience.

99. Cultivate relationships with media outlets or journalists for PR opportunities.

100. Develop a social media content calendar to stay consistent.

101. Encourage customers to leave online reviews or testimonials.

102. Offer personalized packaging or handwritten notes for a

personal touch.

103. Collaborate with influencers or bloggers for product reviews or endorsements.

104. Develop a customer referral program with rewards or discounts.

105. Offer a money-back guarantee or warranty for customer confidence.

106. Participate in online forums or discussion boards to build authority.

107. Utilize customer surveys or polls to gather feedback and insights.

108. Develop partnerships with complementary businesses for cross-promotion.

109. Offer a VIP program with exclusive perks for loyal customers.

110. Leverage video testimonials to build social proof.

111. Develop a customer-centric content marketing strategy.

112. Create a sense of urgency with limited-time sales or discounts.

113. Optimize your website''s user interface and navigation for ease of use.

114. Use retargeting ads to reach customers who have shown interest.

115. Offer live chat support for real-time customer assistance.

116. Collaborate with micro-influencers for cost-effective marketing.

117. Utilize online booking or scheduling tools for service-based businesses.

118. Offer free shipping or flat rate shipping to simplify the buying process.

119. Develop a customer rewards program with points or

discounts.

120. Utilize guest blogging opportunities to reach new audiences.

121. Offer product bundles or gift sets for special occasions.

122. Implement live video streaming to showcase new products or services.

123. Create a sense of community through online forums or groups.

124. Utilize remarketing ads to re-engage with customers who have visited your site.

125. Offer seasonal discounts or promotions to boost sales.

126. Develop strategic partnerships with influencers or bloggers for collaborative campaigns.

127. Optimize your website''s meta tags and descriptions for better search engine visibility.

128. Utilize customer segmentation for personalized marketing campaigns.

129. Offer a free trial or demo of your product or service.

130. Collaborate with local influencers or bloggers for targeted promotion.

131. Create interactive content such as quizzes or contests for customer engagement.

132. Develop a customer feedback or suggestion program for continuous improvement.

133. Utilize influencer marketing to reach niche audiences.

134. Offer a VIP membership program with exclusive benefits.

135. Participate in industry awards or competitions for recognition.

136. Utilize chatbots for 24/7 customer support.

137. Create instructional videos or tutorials to educate customers.

138. Leverage user-generated content for social media campaigns.

139. Offer educational webinars or workshops for industry professionals.

140. Utilize virtual reality or augmented reality experiences for immersive customer interactions.

141. Develop strategic partnerships with non-competing businesses for joint marketing efforts.

142. Create a brand ambassador program for loyal customers.

143. Offer product customization or personalization options.

144. Collaborate with charitable organizations for cause-related marketing initiatives.

145. Utilize influencer takeovers on social media for increased exposure.

146. Host live Q&A sessions or webinars to engage with customers.

147. Offer free or discounted trials for limited periods.

148. Collaborate with local influencers or bloggers for in-person events or meetups.

149. Utilize pop-up shops or temporary retail spaces for physical presence.

150. Develop partnerships with affiliate marketers for increased referral traffic.

151. Offer flash sales or limited-time discounts exclusively for email subscribers.

152. Leverage user-generated content for social proof and authenticity.

153. Develop strategic partnerships with industry experts for co-branded products or services.

154. Create captivating product demo videos to showcase features and benefits.

155. Utilize influencer meetups or events for networking and promotion.

156. Offer early access or exclusive previews for new product releases.

157. Collaborate with local influencers or bloggers for sponsored content in newsletters.

158. Utilize augmented reality or virtual reality experiences for product visualization.

159. Develop partnerships with online influencers for affiliate marketing opportunities.

160. Offer personalized recommendations or product suggestions based on customer preferences.

161. Host live product launch events or webinars for interactive experiences.

162. Utilize influencer podcast sponsorships for targeted advertising.

163. Create interactive quizzes or assessments to engage and educate customers.

164. Establish partnerships with local businesses for joint promotional events or discounts.

165. Offer product subscription services for recurring revenue streams.

166. Utilize SMS marketing for instant customer communication.

167. Develop partnerships with micro-influencers for cost-effective endorsements.

168. Offer exclusive discounts or promotions to social media followers.

169. Collaborate with industry experts for guest blog posts or articles.

170. Utilize influencer social media takeovers to reach new

audiences.

171. Create personalized email marketing campaigns based on customer behavior and preferences.

172. Host live workshops or classes to teach customers new skills or techniques.

173. Offer limited edition or one-time-only products for exclusivity.

174. Utilize influencer product giveaways or contests for increased engagement.

175. Develop partnerships with influencers for co-created content or products.

176. Offer personalized packaging with customer names or messages.

177. Collaborate with local influencers or bloggers for curated gift guides.

178. Utilize interactive video or gamification for customer engagement.

179. Develop partnerships with non-profit organizations for cause-related marketing campaigns.

180. Offer personalized product recommendations based on customer purchase history.

181. Host live online events or webinars with expert guest speakers.

182. Utilize influencer affiliate marketing for increased referral traffic.

183. Create interactive calculators or tools to assist customers in decision-making.

184. Develop partnerships with micro-influencers for cost-effective product testimonials.

185. Offer limited-time collaborations with other brands or designers.

186.   Utilize influencer Instagram Stories or Snapchat takeovers for behind-the-scenes content.

187.   Offer personalized follow-up emails with additional recommendations based on customer purchases.

188. Collaborate with local influencers or bloggers for product styling or fashion lookbooks.

189. Utilize virtual reality or 360-degree videos for immersive product experiences.

190.   Develop partnerships with influencers for co-hosted events or workshops.

191. Offer personalized thank you cards or gifts for customer loyalty.

192. Create exclusive online communities or memberships for premium content or benefits.

193. Utilize influencer partnerships for charitable donations or fundraising initiatives.

194. Offer personalized product bundles based on customer preferences or purchase history.

195. Collaborate with micro-influencers for sponsored posts or product reviews.

196.   Utilize influencer YouTube collaborations for video content creation.

197.   Create interactive quizzes or games to engage and entertain customers.

198. Develop partnerships with influencers for co-branded merchandise or limited editions.

199. Offer personalized styling or home decor consultations for interior design businesses.

200.   Collaborate with local influencers or bloggers for in-store events or pop-up shops.

201. Utilize influencer giveaways or contests for increased

social media engagement.

202. Offer personalized nutrition or fitness plans for health and wellness businesses.

203. Develop partnerships with influencers for co-authored ebooks or digital products.

204. Use virtual reality or augmented reality for virtual showroom experiences.

205. Collaborate with micro-influencers for sponsored Instagram Reels or TikTok videos.

206. Utilize influencers for live demonstration videos or tutorials.

207. Offer personalized services or consultations based on customer needs or goals.

208. Develop partnerships with influencers for co-hosted webinars or online courses.

209. Utilize influencer partnerships for social media influencer takeovers or guest posts.

210. Offer personalized meal plans or recipes for food-related businesses.

211. Collaborate with local influencers or bloggers for product launch events or fashion shows.

212. Utilize influencer collaborations for co-created limited-edition products or collections.

213. Offer personalized skincare or beauty consultations for cosmetic businesses.

214. Develop partnerships with influencers for co-branded podcast episodes or series.

215. Utilize virtual reality or augmented reality for virtual fitting room experiences.

216. Collaborate with micro-influencers for sponsored Pinterest collaborations or boards.

217. Utilize influencer partnerships for guest appearances on YouTube channels or podcasts.

218. Offer personalized travel itineraries or recommendations for travel businesses.

219. Develop partnerships with influencers for co-authored blog posts or ebooks.

220. Utilize influencer collaborations for co-created workshops or online courses.

221. Offer personalized home organization or decluttering services for professional organizers.

222. Collaborate with local influencers or bloggers for product sampling or tasting events.

223. Utilize influencer partnerships for co-hosted Instagram Live sessions or Q&A sessions.

224. Offer personalized financial planning or investment advice for financial businesses.

225. Develop partnerships with influencers for co-branded merchandise or fashion lines.

226. Utilize virtual reality or augmented reality for virtual home staging or design consultations.

227. Collaborate with micro-influencers for sponsored Facebook Live events or streaming.

228. Utilize influencer collaborations for co-created fitness or workout programs.

229. Offer personalized coaching or mentorship for professional development businesses.

230. Develop partnerships with influencers for co-authored white papers or research papers.

231. Utilize influencer collaborations for co-created art or design collections.

232. Offer personalized pet training or behavior consultations

for pet-related businesses.

233. Collaborate with local influencers or bloggers for sponsored retreats or wellness events.

234. Utilize influencer partnerships for co-hosted cooking or baking classes.

235. Offer personalized wedding planning or event coordination services for event planners.

236. Develop partnerships with influencers for co-branded recipe books or cookbooks.

237. Utilize virtual reality or augmented reality for virtual fitness or wellness experiences.

238. Collaborate with micro-influencers for sponsored Twitter chats or Twitter takeovers.

239. Utilize influencer collaborations for co-created mindfulness or meditation programs.

240. Offer personalized language lessons or tutoring for education businesses.

241. Develop partnerships with influencers for co-authored self-help or motivational books.

242. Utilize influencer partnerships for co-hosted DIY or craft workshops.

243. Offer personalized business coaching or consulting for business coaches.

244. Collaborate with local influencers or bloggers for sponsored adventure or travel experiences.

245. Utilize influencer collaborations for co-created gardening or plant care guides.

246. Offer personalized therapy or counseling sessions for mental health businesses.

247. Develop partnerships with influencers for co-branded tech gadgets or accessories.

248. Utilize virtual reality or augmented reality for virtual therapy or coaching sessions.

249. Collaborate with micro-influencers for sponsored beauty or product tutorials on Instagram Stories.

250. Utilize influencer partnerships for co-hosted motivational or personal development webinars.

Remember to customize these tips based on your specific industry and goals. Good luck with your small business!